Message of the Moment

Inspirational Thoughts of the Moment for the Moment

By
Lisa J. Smith

Peeps Publishing
PP

Detroit, MI
Edition 1
2013

Other books by Lisa J. Smith:

36 Months
3 Years of Healing Through Social Media Posts

Peeps Publishing
PP
Detroit, MI
2012

Message of the Moment
Inspirational Thoughts of the Moment for the Moment

By Lisa J. Smith

Published and distributed by Peeps Publishing
Detroit, MI

Contact publisher for orders
www.peepspublishing.com

The author of this book does not dispense medical or mental health information. The author is merely stating her opinions and thoughts and it is not to be used as a substitute for any medical, emotional, psychological, or physical care. The intent of the author is to offer information of a general nature to uplift and inspire. It does not substitute for any health care for anyone. If you choose to use any of this book for your own personal well being, it is at your own free will and risk and the author is not, and will not be held responsible for your actions.

ISBN-10: 0985144831
ISBN-13: 978-0-9851448-3-8

Library of Congress Control Number: 2013914216

Peeps Publishing
PP

Detroit, MI

Acknowledgments and Dedication

This book would not have been possible without the support and encouragement of each one of you. Without your support and willingness to learn, grow, share, connect, and heal there would be no me. Words can't express my gratitude to you as we continue on this interesting journey of humanity that I often refer to as the "magic carpet ride".

I would like to express my gratitude to the people who saw me through this book; to all those who provided support, talked things over, offered comments, and assisted in the follow through of the details.

I dedicate this to all the people who inspired these messages of the moments. From coworkers, family, listeners, old friends and new friends, clients, energies in all forms, and the people I meet everyday who get up to face a new day, even on the toughest of days, you've inspired me. You've all been my teachers and I am forever grateful for the lessons and connections, regardless of how short or how long, painful or joyful, they may have been.

As always to my awesome, beautiful, and wise Allie and Andrew, thank you for being my teachers'. You're the light of my life. Knowing you and being your mom is *my* honor and privilege. The love I have for you is beyond words. There is no distance that will ever separate us from the bond that we have.

Steve, thank you for all the hours of patience you show me everyday, especially while I endlessly worked on my lap top while you were hungry. Thank you for listening to me go on, and on, and loving me no matter what. Your support and patience with me everyday has showed me what true friendship and love really is. You're the "best friend" a girl could ever have.

My mom always taught me, "There's nothing you can't do when you set your mind to it". Thank you for always being my cheerleader and helping me to see the light at the end of the tunnel when I couldn't see it myself. Your belief in me has stuck more than you know. To my Dad, thank you for teaching me what a *warrior* really is and for teaching me the value of the word "should". You taught me, through your actions, what hard work, respect, perseverance, and dedication is. What a valuable lesson to learn through your examples of being and doing, not just saying.

Introduction

Do you ever feel like you just need a sign that you're on the right track? Do you ever feel that you're all alone swimming in an ocean with completely strange people; all of who you think might be nuttier than you? Do you ever feel like you're misunderstood and left out? What about missing something or the feeling that there must be more?

Well, if you're like the rest of us, I'm sure you answered yes to most of the questions. After years of working with people on the air, in groups and privately, the one thing I've learned is we're all in the same boat. This boat floats in a sea of uncertainty; of our purpose, our journey, our decisions and choices, and most of all, of who we really are.

From the work I do as an intuitive, I've learned that people basically ask the same questions in a million different ways, and how I can answer them. Think of the human experience like this; there are seven billion separate people on the planet. No two of us are exactly the same. We all have our own look, personality, experiences, history, and each has our own journey. I believe at a non-physical level we all come from "one". We could debate what to call the "one", or if there is really is a "one", but my belief is we all come from the "one", whatever that may be. We're having individual physical experiences, while having a collective non-physical experience, all at the same time.

Think of the scene in the movie, "Willie Wonka", where he transports a chocolate bar over their heads into billions of little pieces. Yep, there you have it. We're all a chocolate bar. The bar goes from one to billions; the same bar having billions of different experiences, in different places in the room, yet still being a piece of the *same* chocolate bar. I've explained this to people over the years and every time I do, I feel them get an *a-ha moment,* their energy shifts, and the light bulb goes off. It helps to have a visual and movies are great teachers.

So, with the thousands of messages I have given to so many different people around the world, the underlying issues always come down to the same old thing for most of us in our core, our self worth. From our self worth stems setting boundaries, using our voice, the disease to please, forgiveness, being powerful, creating change, letting go, acceptance, self love, etc.

Just think, if your self worth has been in the pooper from years of self abuse, (self abuse because we know it's called 'self' for a reason and we're responsible for our own feelings and perceptions) we have an extremely difficult time remembering who we are let alone how powerful we were created to be. We become fearful of our power, fearful of change, fearful of love, fearful of what people think of us, afraid of people not liking us, disempowered, confused, weak, etc.

Whew! That's a lot of stuff going on right there. I see it happening over and over, and over, again with everyone. It happened to me and most likely, if you're reading this, you're right along with us. At least we're all together.

Hey, that's ok! We're here to live, have experiences, fall down, and forget who we are. Then through the help of each other and our own self work, we lift ourselves up and keep going until we *do* remember who we are. For some that might take awhile, if ever. That's ok because that's their journey and it's on *their* time schedule, not ours. For others who are willing to open themselves up, take a risk, do their work, and believe that somehow, someway there's more to it then we see, it may not be easy, yet the path to self worth and self discovery will be very rewarding.

"When the student is ready the teacher will teach". When you begin to retrain your brain, therefore your thoughts and old beliefs about yourself, you can begin to shift your attention onto what you want, not that of what others want for you. When you know you can shift your attention and focus, you can then rise up to meet your power. Your state of previous self worth will be changed to that of love, not fear. Your conditioned and self abusive thoughts can be reconditioned into; powerful, full, beautiful, confident, thoughts of self love and inner beauty.

Sometimes all we need is a little validation that we're on the right track and that *all is as it shall be.* These messages are really nothing new and you may have heard them before. The difference is they're finding their way to you *now.* They're written with a different flare that will hopefully trigger an *aha moment* that will enable you to see yourself, others, and life through different eyes.

In this book, you'll find inspirational and motivational thoughts written to; inspire, uplift, connect, and remind you of the most important thing in the world, YOU!

Whether you read this book straight through, use it as a daily reminder, or pick it up randomly through out the day and open it to the message that you need to hear at that moment, you'll be sure to find a positive and affirming message just for you. These messages came to me after meeting with clients, having my own less than favorable days, and meeting with strangers on the street for random inspiring conversations. They are meant to be shared.

The greatest gift you can give yourself is the gift of self acceptance, therefore self love. When you can accept yourself as the perfectly imperfect, magical being that you were created to be, just like the rest of us, you'll then know that there is *no way* your worth is not priceless. When you know your self worth, you'll carry on accordingly.

I always say, "Information leads to knowledge, and knowledge leads to wisdom". You'll have the information that you are; strong, wise, and beautiful. You'll have the knowledge that we're all created as one being having 7 billion different experiences at the same time. Now allow your wisdom to guide you to *your* truths. Be your own advocate, trust yourself, come from your adult with your actions and smart choices, and allow your inner child to; love, be playful, have compassion for self, and feel joy. Allow your light to shine bright.

You're in there somewhere waiting to be self loved. The first step is beginning to *believe* you're worthy of such greatness and love, and then to *know* you're worthy of your own self love. The truth is, you always have, and already do know this in your heart, which is why you feel the emptiness at times that you feel. That emptiness, disconnect, and the longing for you is you missing you.

Allow these messages to be your *a-ha moment* when you're ready. Everything is only a moment changing and shifting form. As the wind changes easily and effortlessly on a beautiful spring day, so do the energies among us. The messages in this book capture a moment of time meant for you now. Let theses messages open your heart to the power of you, the beauty of others, as well as the magnificence of life.

What are *your* messages of the moment? How are *you* going to share them with the world?

With much love and gratitude,

Lisa J.

VII

Message of the Moment

Inspirational Thoughts of the Moment for the Moment

Acceptance - 6

Dreams - 53, 203

Awareness - 64 **By**

Vase - 89 **Lisa J. Smith**

Forgiveness - 78-9
TRust - 92
Appreciate - 99
Being 101
Enough 113
Align 258

11, 12, 14, 15, 21, 25, (31), 35, (36), (41)
46, (49), (54), 67, (69), 83, (88), (94), 96
(102), 130, 143, (145), 155, (157), (162)
(177), 185, (187), 196, 197, 224
237, 272, (273), (277)

Today

Message of the Moment:

Know and *set* your intention and *allow* the universe to rise up to meet it.

It'll never let you down.

Your job is to *know* yourself and what you want your life to look like it.

Life is by your design.

Don't worry about the universe, it already knows you.

It always has and always will!

♥LjS

1

Message of the Moment:

The best part of going through growing pains is the wisdom that comes out the other side.

I.e., Seeing people for what they are and not allowing them to take your power any longer.

♥ LjS

Message of the Moment:

Seeing your potential + someone to show you your potential
(although never easy seeing it) = best gift ever.

Once seen, it can forever change your life if you allow it too.

♥ LjS

Message of the Moment:

Don't allow the journey of others to become the journey of you.

♥LjS

Message of the Moment:

Unless you're going to do it the *right way*,
whatever that way is for you,
don't do it at all.

Mistakes allowed and encouraged.

There IS a difference.

♥LjS

Message of the Moment:

ACCEPTANCE:

*Allowing Clear Channels Employing Patience Totally Acknowledging Now
Completely Ever-after*

♥LjS

Message of the Moment:

People will only do what you allow them to do.

♥LjS

Message of the Moment:

We all worry about our loved ones crossing over, dying or changing form.

This is what I've learned:

Have you ever seen a baby born who's not crying and doesn't look scared of their new unknown world?

NO!
They cry, scream, and look terrified.

Now, have you ever seen anyone kicking and screaming like a newborn baby when they die?

NO!
We die in peace and we're calm, regardless of how we die (or change form).

Maybe birth is what's so tough… not death.

Maybe birth is death and death is birth?

Maybe the worry when someone dies is our own fear of death and the unknown, not the fear for our loved ones after all.

♥LjS

Message of the Moment:

There's only one destination...the ways in which you get there are infinite.

You choose the path.

The destination *is what it is*.

We'll only truly understand this when we no longer are in the physical form.

There's no way to comprehend this while we live within the confides of what we think while in our humanity.

♥LjS

Message of the Moment:

It's really all about YOU...everything you do is about YOU!

Make your life your own, not what other people want it to look like.

You already own your life, now become aware and present with it.

Don't wait until you look back and say,
"What just happened?! It really was about me after all".

♥LjS

Message of the Moment:

You can't trust others until you learn to trust and believe in yourself.

See yourself as valuable.

Know your truth.

Trust your intuition…we ALL have it.

Now believe you are worthy of your greatest dreams.

When you do this you'll find what you've been looking for along, YOU!

♥ LjS

Message of the Moment:

Everyone talks about "manifesting".

They're too busy worrying about what they don't have, to see what they
DO HAVE!

Gratitude for what we do have opens doors.

The want, which is the alignment of lack in disguise, closes them.

♥ LjS

Message of the Moment:

Never assume those you do "business" with are your friends.

Friends and "friendly" are two completely different things.

Sounds easy, yet for many this is a tough lesson to learn.

Learning it now will save you a lot of disappointment later.

♥LjS

Message of the Moment:

Accepting EACH moment as it comes;
this just might be a key to allowing the inner peace we all seek.

♥LjS

Message of the Moment:

Realism and idealism are two different things.

We tend to get them mixed up and end up living in misery.

Realism is what is...idealism is what you wish they were.

Which do you think is easier to REALLY live within?

♥LjS

Message of the Moment:

Sometimes people question why they had to be born.

They already know the answer.

Sometimes the answers aren't the easy ones, yet the ones they need to know.

♥LjS

Message of the Moment:

I've learned that in the end nothing is what you think it will be about.

It's all about something you'll never understand until you're there.

♥LjS

Message of the Moment:

You can plan with the best of intentions all you want,
yet sometimes what you plan for is not the plan at all.

♥LjS

Message of the Moment:

Listening to your heart doesn't mean doing what you want, when you want.

Listening to your heart is being in the flow even when you don't like it.

♥LjS

Message of the Moment:

No one said you have to like everything all the time.

♥LjS

Message of the Moment:

The only truth there is, is the truth you tell yourself.

♥ LjS

Message of the Moment:

People behave the way *they* want and choose too...
not the way *you* want and choose for them to behave.

♥LjS

Message of the Moment:

Just because one is "spiritual" doesn't mean they are not prone to human mistakes. We often turn those who write books, the ones we turn into gurus, and the self proclaimed professionals and experts into perfect people. There's no *perfect* for anyone who has ever walked this planet. There are humans having experiences. All of us are imperfect. If someone proclaims their perfection, then you must know they are the ones who are far from it.

 LjS

Message of the Moment:

BRING IT ON:

*Beautiful Radiating Iridescent Nothingness Glowing
In Terrific Omnipresence Now*

♥LjS

Message of the Moment:

Sometimes all you can do is get over it.

♥LjS

Message of the Moment:

Live from the end

♥LjS

Message of the Moment:

L_____O_____V_____E_____

♥LjS

Message of the Moment:

Sometimes it doesn't matter how hard you try,
in the end it will be what it will be.

Only you choose what that will be.

♥LjS

Message of the Moment:

Legacy...

What do you want yours to be?

How are you behaving?
What are you doing to create that?
Are your actions stronger than your words?

Your character becomes your legacy.

How are you living today,
to be what you would like your legacy to look like tomorrow?

♥ LjS

Message of the Moment:

A reminder that you always need your own advice.

LjS

Message of the Moment:

Amazing how life can transform you.

Sometimes it feels good and sometimes it feels, not so good.

Either way, *TRANSFORMATION* is the only way to evolve.

Learn to say,

"Bring it on,
gently with ease and grace please"!

♥LjS

Message of the Moment:

When you admit to yourself that you don't know everything, maybe even that you know very little, you'll be wise, not smart.

♥LjS

Message of the Moment:

You have this time to do whatever you want with it.

The time is yours.

♥LjS

Message of the Moment:

There's beauty in both sides of light and dark.

It's up to you to use the tools you have in your tool box to see it.

♥LjS

Message of the Moment:

Those who seek answers find questions.

Those who ask questions find answers.

LjS

Message of the Moment:

The creation of you is priceless.

Did you know that?

I bet if you did, you would be nicer to yourself today and everyday!

♥LjS

Message of the Moment:

You're the only enemy you have.

Everyone else is a reminder of where you are on your journey, what you need to look at more closely, and what you need to release.

♥ LjS

Message of the Moment:

When holding your conviction, hold it from your love and your truth, not your defensiveness.

Being defensive is coming from fear, not love.

Know love

Fear is not real

Only the fear of the fear is real

♥LjS

Message of the Moment:

When you are comfortable with your choices and decisions, therefore yourself, there's no need to justify yourself to anyone, ever again.

♥ LjS

Message of the Moment:

Check yourself to see where you are right now?

How do you feel?

Is everything ok, right now, in this moment as you read this?

OK...breathe.

See, you're ok.

You'll always be ok.

♥LjS

Message of the Moment:

Faith is an old friend that will find you.

Open your door, put the welcome mat out, and be ready for a visit from a long lost friend.

The truth is Faith never left you...maybe you're the one that left Faith.

Maybe the welcome mat is actually out for you.

♥LjS

Message of the Moment:

Going back to where you started from is always a good idea.

The answers may be there.

Let's see what happens next.

The truth is, the way it's working might not be working so well after all, so what do you have to lose?

♥LjS

Message of the Moment:

Watching the incense burn,
the smoke dance through the warm breeze.

If we only could be like the smoke.
Leaving our source and going wherever the breeze takes us...

No expectations of where we're going…

Dancing effortlessly through the air twisting and turning...

Going wherever we go...

Simplicity and movement at its finest...

Life!

♥ LjS

Message of the Moment:

And *ALL* is as it needs to be.

Everything is a much greater design and bigger picture.

What is happening to you right now, and who you are, is only one piece of a massive beautiful puzzle.

We each make up one piece of that puzzle.

The puzzle would not be complete or nearly as beautiful without your piece or mine.

The one piece never sees the whole picture, it only completes it.

Remember that!

♥ LjS

Message of the Moment:

If something isn't in your best interest; leave it be, keep walking, and you'll find yourself wherever you find yourself to be next.

It'll be better there.

Trust the process.

♥LjS

Message of the Moment:

Sometimes people think they know what's best for you...
If you listen to your heart, trust yourself, and recognize your own knowing,
maybe just maybe, you'll find only you know what's best for you.

♥LjS

Message of the Moment:

If you find that something is missing inside your heart....
Maybe it's a fight worth fighting for to find out what it is!

Believe that it's important.

LjS

Message of the Moment:

If the miracle of infinite musical possibilities is possible,
anything can be possible.

Believe only in what you know to be possible for you.

The rest is a distraction!

♥LjS

Message of the Moment:

Sometimes you just have to say,
"I'm not afraid anymore" and move on.

♥ LjS

Message of the Moment:

A law of physics:
Every action has an equal and opposite reaction.

Maybe we need to start thinking how our actions cause reactions in others.

Sometimes good...sometimes NOT so good

Choose care-full-y!

There are no re-do's and the damage can be done before you know what happened.

Become aware of your actions.

Your actions will create your future.

♥LjS

Message of the Moment:

Disappointment...

An appointment that has been *dissed*

♥LjS

Message of the Moment:

Next time someone *should's* on you say,

"Did you should on me?" and watch their reaction.

The word "should" takes away your power and your choices.

Don't should on others and don't let them should on you.

♥LjS

Message of the Moment:

When you give up on your dreams…

You give up on living.

♥LjS

Message of the Moment:

The balance of the universe...

To receive one must give and to give one must receive.

♥LjS

Message of the Moment:

The world is full of takers.

They'll take only take what you allow them to take.

Be your own advocate.

Trust yourself.

Leave the takers behind.

Walk freely into your destiny, whatever that may be,
and wherever that takes you.

♥LjS

Message of the Moment:

Trust your heart and know that you're safe.

♥LjS

Message of the Moment:

It's a new day.

Do you ever stop to think that time waits for no one?

What are you waiting for?

♥ LjS

Message of the Moment:

The path to "enlightenment" is not obtained easily...

Although "easy" can only defined by you.

♥LjS

Message of the Moment:

When someone pushes your buttons, and triggers you every time, you have to realize that the *point* of the trigger is to cause a reaction?

That reaction to the trigger is what brings you to your wake up moment and that moment brings you a choice.

The choice of, "Do I allow this pain or not"?

In that moment, you have a choice and that choice brings you to where you are now.

Where are you?
Do you feel the point?

When you no longer feel the point, the trigger will be gone.

♥LjS

Message of the Moment:

Remove the thoughts and inner beliefs that tell you what you *think* you are, and become what you *KNOW* you are.

♥ LjS

Message of the Moment:

They used to think bumblebees couldn't fly, we now know that isn't true.

This is proof that anything is possible.

The fact that we even know this now proves that too!

Think about it, you never know what is possible until you drill down, examine things more closely, and then let the truth show you its truth.

Truths come in many forms, yet there is always one truth.

LjS

Message of the Moment:

All I'm going to say is this…

If you think for one second you're doing it alone,
I'm living proof, right here and now, telling you that you're not.

It amazes me everyday, in every moment,
of how much there really is going on always.

The messages and answers you seek are everywhere, all the time.

There is no alone.

All you have to do is pay attention and listen to everything and nothing at all.

♥ LjS

Message of the Moment:

You're not what people label you...

You're what you label you!

♥ LjS

Message of the Moment:

AWARENESS:

*A*lways *W*orking *A*t Remembering *E*asily *N*ow *E*venly *S*ilently *S*hifting

♥LjS

Message of the Moment:

Why do we struggle?

Because we learned a long time ago that within the struggle there's movement.

We like things that move.

What we forgot is that before we learned about struggle, we learned the more we resist the more *it'll* persist.

Funny how we forget the first things we actually really *knew*.

♥ LjS

Message of the Moment:

If you want to be loved you must be love to others.

LjS

Message of the Moment:

When we surrender to "what is," and allow
"what is" to do its thing, we finally find internal peace.

The struggle to fight through the illusion that we believed is there,
is no longer there.

We don't surrender because we're in fear and are weak.

We surrender because we're tired of the fight.

The reality is we have finally won the battle.

True strength lies is the surrender.

Weakness lies in the battle.

LjS

Message of the Moment:

By the time you read this, the true moment is gone.

We're actually always living somewhere in the past.

While we exist in the physical world, it's simply impossible to be in the time of *what is* when in *real time*.

If you're living in the past with things in your life...then you're living in the past, past, past.

Chew on that!

Seems kind of silly to let those things dictate our future, huh?

♥LjS

Message of the Moment:

The universe takes the most unlikely people and uses them in the most extraordinary ways.

♥LjS

Message of the Moment:

You inspire me.

Thank you!

♥LjS

Message of the Moment:

The blessing comes in realizing you are, and always have been, blessed by all that is, and ever was, and will be forever.

You can't be separate from what you are and what is.

 LjS

Message of the Moment:

I always say,

"There's a lot of value in change".

Don't ever under estimate the value of a $penny$.

All the little *change* adds up to a lot of *value*.

What a metaphor!

♥LjS

Message of the Moment:

Did you know the messages in music and lyrics are telling you stories?

Are you paying attention?

What are they telling you?

♥LjS

Message of the Moment:

Phone lines open...

We're listening.

Aren't you glad to know someone is?

♥LjS

Message of the Moment:

Aren't we all just misfits trying to fit into places we want to belong,
yet maybe just don't fit?

It's only when we realize we are misfits do we truly begin to fit.

Go figure!

♥LjS

Message of the Moment:

At the core we understand people; on the surface at times it seems impossible.

Here is some help:

"God grant me the serenity
to accept the things I cannot change;
courage to change the things I can;
and wisdom to know the difference".
--*Reinhola Niebuhr*

♥LjS

Message of the Moment:

Patience with life

♥ LjS

Message of the Moment:

Someone asked me my thoughts on forgiveness in a session today.
Although it's never easy and a very difficult thing to do,
forgiveness is always for us, not the other person.
This is some of what I told them.

1. Realizing you're not a victim and nothing happened to you.

2. Their actions are a result of their behaviors and choices, not yours.

3. The issues that result from their actions are nothing more than issues that needed to be resolved in the first place. Finding gratitude for them being brought to the surface is important. This way you can revisit them, look at them differently, heal them once and for all, and let them go.

4. Knowing that they'll always be who they are, and accepting them for who they are, is very different then accepting the behavior.

5. Being grateful for the issues that come up because they are acting as a mirror and showing us what *we* need to look at it within ourselves to heal.

6. The only actions you can be responsible for are you own. Accepting, forgiving, and being easy on yourself are the ways you'll find peace.

7. Acceptance (which doesn't mean approving) of any and all actions is the key to healing all wounds, moving forward, and living in peace.

8. Forgiveness can be ongoing. It doesn't mean you failed if you're angry. It doesn't mean things are your fault. It doesn't mean that you're not getting what forgiveness means. It means that's life, people are people, and through living, we hurt others and we get hurt. That's what it means.

9. We're human and part of this experience is to feel the humanity and forgiveness is part of humanity. If we didn't need to learn it we wouldn't have to be here.

10. The fact is, the people who hurt you the most, on some level, must be the ones who love you the most. It's never easy to hurt people although sometimes some people make it look awful easy. One day you'll see!

REMEMBER, FORGIVING IS AN ACT FOR YOU, NOT FOR OTHERS

The people you're forgiving do not need to hear it from you
for you to *feel* it for them.

The chances are good they won't get what you are forgiving anyways,
because if they were able to *get it*,
they wouldn't have hurt you in the first place!

♥LjS

Message of the Moment:

A dragonfly from 300 million years ago was the size of a hawk.

Amazing, simply, amazing!

Imagine in 300 million years what size you'll be.

♥LjS

Message of the Moment:

First and only step to forgiveness is the
desire, want, and the NEED to forgive.

If you're having a hard time forgiving,
then you must not want it badly enough...

IT'S ALL ABOUT YOU!

♥LjS

Message of the Moment:

You never know how *light* you can travel,
until you dump everything you're carrying.

♥LjS

Message of the Moment:

Today is so beautiful.

Can you see it?

It's up to you to change your view, therefore your perspective,
in order to see it.

It'll wait for you.

♥ LjS

Message of the Moment:

Do what you *LOVE*...

Be the rock star that you are by living in *your* heart, not someone else's.

♥ LjS

Message of the Moment:

New day sunshine

The day is waiting for you

Make it your own

♥LjS

Message of the Moment:

The truth of the matter is not everyone is your friend,
not everyone will care about you when you need them to care about you,
and those people who hurt you are still as important as the few who never will.

Great, huh!

In the end...does it even really matter?

No

What matters is what you do with them while you still have them
and how lovingly you can let them go.

♥LjS

Message of the Moment:

Being positive is the new way of
becoming the most popular kid in school.

Listen up...you're human right now.

Good days and bad days, no one is positive 100% of the time.

You have to know one way of being to know the other.
That's by design, ya know!

Just be ok with who YOU are, right now.

Don't worry about getting it right and being perfect...
that's the illusion, you'll only feel like you failed.

Being positive is accepting *all* of your humanity in *all of* your moments.

Be your own truth.

♥LjS

Message of the Moment:

Listen...

Let's be honest…

Just do the best you can and let the chips fall where they may.

If you don't like where they end up...clean them up and start over!

♥LjS

Message of the Moment:

Once upon a time, we all loved a beautiful and priceless vase because of its flawless beauty. We saw it as perfect with no defects. One day the vase broke and it was no longer as beautiful as it once was. After it was glued back together, it just didn't have the same perceived perfection and beauty as it once did. The vase didn't think it was loved anymore because it wasn't perfect, so it lost its shine. The less shiny it was, the less people loved it, and the less people who loved it, the less it loved itself.

The funny thing is about a vase that was once perfect, and now imperfect, is that the imperfections of the glued vase make it a unique vase unlike any others. Before it broke, it was beautiful and perfect, yet not beautifully unique.

Moral of the story: It's often the imperfections we find in ourselves, as well as in each other, that make us the most beautiful and certainly the most unique. The shine comes from within and is what attracts others to see the beauty of what is, not what they want it to be.

Leonardo da Vinci's Mona Lisa is not what we consider "beautiful", yet is one of the most stunning paintings in history, she shines!

♥LjS

Message of the Moment:

Actually, you're never really learning anything new...

You're just being validated for what you already DO know!

♥LjS

Message of the Moment:

If you want the whole truth and the entire story, sometimes you have to dig a little deeper within the details to find it.

Nothing is as it appears.

As you move through out your day today, try to look past what you obviously see and look beyond the surface.

You never know what treasures you'll find below the tip of the iceberg.

♥LjS

Message of the Moment:

Trust:

Something that people worship when it's real
and reel from when it's broken.

♥LjS

Message of the Moment:

I saw this on a sign…

"Home is where your story begins"
Author Unknown

Your story starts right now…
I guess you've always been home.

♥LjS

Message of the Moment:

Do you ever feel like you're in the circus and there are a bunch of little clowns running around you trying to put out fires?

I do too.

It's ok, they really are running around.

Just move out of their way…it's easier for you that way.

♥LjS

Message of the Moment:

Be sure to spend a second saying thank you to the sky above and the Earth below for all they do for you!

Hug a tree, kiss the ground, and praise the sky for they sustain and nourish the soul.

Without them there would be no you.

♥ LjS

Message of the Moment:

Just because you can doesn't mean you "should"!

♥ LjS

Message of the Moment:

Start thinking of the world;
it's way bigger than you can imagine,
and way smaller than you can imagine, all at the same time.

♥LjS

Message of the Moment:

Realism vs. Idealism Lesson #73:

Some things are just meant to be what they are.

They might not be *ideal* for you, yet are *real* for a reason.

That's the lesson.

♥LjS

Message of the Moment

Sometimes it feels like no matter how many doors are given, it's that many more doors that slam shut.

When those days feel hopeless, it's important to remember you're not what you do, the experiences you've had, the doors that have slammed shut, the doors that have opened, or the people who have come into your life; good, bad or indifferent.

YOU ARE YOU, beautiful, unique, and priceless all by your lonesome.

The doors, people, opportunities (or lack thereof), and experiences are *not* what matters.

YOU matter and you matter to those who appreciate you.

Now, you have to appreciate you.

By the way, maybe there really are no doors?

Maybe you can't find them because they're not there in the first place?

Ponder that!

♥ LjS

99

Message of the Moment:

The only way to see the light is to know the dark.

Don't over react in either direction.

One is not better than the other.

Both are equally important.

Allow them to help you find balance.

♥LjS

Message of the Moment:

The goal is not to be one...we already are one.

The goal is to *realize* that we already ARE one.

When we know this, those who wish to bring forth more love, greater awareness, inner and outer peace, healing, wisdom etc., will know that their *being it* changes the collective whole for all.

Being is as *important* as doing

♥LjS

Message of the Moment:

If you don't believe...who will?

♥LjS

Message of the Moment:

Ok this is the deal:

If you ask enough people the SAME questions, hoping to hear what you want to hear, you'll finally find the answers you're looking for.

It's that simple.

You'll get what you want, but is it really what you need?

Maybe what you're actually getting is what you have been asking for all along?

♥ LjS

Message of the Moment:

Shooting yourself in the foot, as they say,
always ends up backfiring into way more than your foot!

Better not to shoot and just walk away.

Some things are better left un-fired!

Wisdom tells us this.

♥LjS

Message of the Moment:

Affirmation:

"I would like to give thanks the relationships over the past few years that have been lost. I would like to thank each one of you. For within my loss, I have found my soul, regained my power, and rediscovered my courage and my strength.
Thank you for being a teacher.
Thank you for being a friend.
We're all teachers to each other".

Who are your teachers?

Be sure to find gratitude for them in your heart.
They did a lot more for you than you will ever know.

♥LjS

Message of the Moment:

The goal of a master warrior is to turn the energy of a huge disappointment into a far more successful endeavor than the disappointment itself would have ever brought.

♥LjS

Message of the Moment:

The middle is up to you.

♥LjS

Message of the Moment:

Just because the world hasn't heard of you,
doesn't mean you haven't done great things.

It does mean however, that the great things you've done
have been heard by those who were made greater by hearing what you said.

Too many people get the above confused.

♥LjS

Message of the Moment:

Gifts are sometimes given in the most backwards of ways.

It's only when you start to lose your gift do you realize that what you had along was really a gift in the first place.

I.e. being afraid of ones power, strength, and courage.

♥ LjS

Message of the Moment:

I suppose just take a step in the right direction.

A million tiny steps will lead to a great big giant one, huh?

♥LjS

Message of the Moment:

Affirmation:

"I believe we need the absence of all to see the light of all....just because I believe that, doesn't mean I have to like it...it just means *it is what it is.*

Knowing that takes the edge off.

Being everything, always at once, is what I've always been, always am, and always will be.

Boxing with everything and everyone to be right and to make a point, is boxing with me and comes from ego.

Today, I choose to value myself and my energy more.
I will put gloves down and just be me".

♥ LjS

Message of the Moment:

Baseball bats
We use them to beat ourselves up.

Give them up…
Stop swinging…
Let them go…

Dig down deep and transmute each one of your bats.

YOU DON'T NEED THEM ANYMORE!

They're used for hitting balls, not for hitting ourselves.

♥ LjS

Message of the Moment:

There is always enough.

When you know this you will be set free.

You'll know that when you feel your worth.

Be your worth.

Be free from what you think you are, and believe in what you're born to be.

♥LjS

Message of the Moment:

Create a rock star wall…

"If you say you want to be a rock star, then go ahead and be one"

(Insert picture here)

Yep, that simple, at least for today!

♥LjS

Message of the Moment:

The beauty of a flower:

Pushing through the soil only to emerge as a wondrous miracle.
A flower; full of life, freshness, color, strength, and fragrance.

The beauty of *you*!

Become the flower and allow your roots to root
and your flower to blossom...

This is your moment.

Seize it, rise up, show it, live it, be it!

♥ LjS

Message of the Moment:

Don't let other peoples illusions ruin it for you.

It's tough enough to not let your own illusions ruin it for you.

♥LjS

Message of the Moment:

Call a re-do, it's ok!

We all get them when it comes to ourselves…it's called a new day!

The beauty is we get a lot of chance's to get it right
and no one's keeping score.

♥LjS

Message of the Moment:

Make it a point to end your day knowing something you didn't know when you woke up today.

♥LjS

Message of the Moment:

Luckiest person in the world...

Yep, Y O U!

Maybe say blessed instead.

♥LjS

Message of the Moment:

And tomorrow is Monday AGAIN.

There'll come a time when you'll look forward to this "AGAIN" thing.

Make that day today, and there will be no "AGAIN" in your Monday.

♥LjS

Message of the Moment:

Don't wish for those things you truly don't know or haven't yet experienced.

They never look like what you expect or want them too anyway.

Sometimes better, sometimes worse, always different!

Allow "what is" into the moment and let be what might be.

There's always something around the next corner.

If you're always wishing, wanting, and hoping,
you're doing that rather than just
allowing what is natural and in divine order *to be*.

LjS

Message of the Moment:

Each one of us has the ability to actually be whatever we want to be...

Most of us don't even bother tapping into our potential
(for the various reasons we use to stay defeated and small).

Don't be the person, who does not,

Be the person that did.

♥LjS

Message of the Moment:

It's funny how lessons just sneak up on you when you least expect them, from the least likely people and places, in all kinds of forms, neither good nor bad, just there for the learning.

♥LjS

Message of the Moment:

Starting over is never easy.

But then again, fighting for what you need never is.

It's the things that are the most valuable that cost us the most.

♥LjS

Message of the Moment:

The things we don't do for our dreams.

What have you done for yours today?

♥ LjS

Message of the Moment:

Breathe and put one foot in front of the other.

One foot...one foot...next foot...one foot...

Breathe...

One foot

Breathe

♥LjS

Message of the Moment:

Are you the master or servant over your life?

♥ LjS

Message of the Moment:

Illuminate your mind.

In other words, start turning things on!

♥LjS

Message of the Moment:

Accept the fact that you don't know everything
and let life bring you what you need...

Stop fighting for what you want and allow what you need to heal you.

You may be surprised that what you need is
far greater than what you *thought* you wanted.

The path has led you here, right now.

Accept that and allow life to be ok.

You don't have to fight everything.

LjS

Message of the Moment:

Reflection is a beautiful thing.

It shows us the image of what we're seeing yet that reflection is backwards (or forwards) to give us a different perspective so that we can see both sides.

This is wisdom.
This is learning.

This subtle, yet beautiful, teacher is a gift.

Be grateful for this ability.

It's in the reflection, without you even seeing it, you see exactly who you are, where you need to be going, and what you are and are not.

The beauty of all that is!

♥LjS

Message of the Moment:

Spirit therapy...

Allow it!

Call it what you want

♥ LjS

Message of the Moment:

One day...
everyone is going to be surprised or not surprised at all.

♥LjS

Message of the Moment:

Be full in your presence
Be aware of your body in space
Breathe
Own your space
Love that in which you are right now
Remember, you are loved.

LjS

Message of the Moment:

If you know something in your heart and you believe it 100%…become it.

It's there for a reason.

Spirit doesn't understand the words,
"No, not, can't, but, next time, maybe, someday, no way, if", etc.

They tell me, "That does not compute".

They also don't understand asking for more money…they don't know what
that is either.

Money is a human thing.
Try asking and confirming (a.k.a. knowing) that *all* your needs are met in this
moment, and will always be met, for all your days to come.

That they'll understand.

♥LjS

Message of the Moment:

What does "spirit" mean to you?

There's no right and wrong.

♥LjS

Message of the Moment:

Remember there is NO letting go.

There's only accepting and letting be.

Keep it simple.

♥LjS

Message of the Moment:

Don't let the copy cats in life get you down.

You know *your* own truth and that's all that matters.

Be *you* and don't worry about *them*.

Let them figure it out for themselves however they can.

Stay in your own cup!

 LjS

Message of the Moment:

Eat when you're hungry.

Cry when you want to be sad.

Laugh when you're joyful.

Sleep when you're tired.

Be in peace when you want solitude.

Be what you want to be when you want to be it...and walk on!

It's all just a moment.

♥LjS

Message of the Moment:

It's HAPPY hour!

Yippee!!!

Smile because someone is thinking of you right now.

I guarantee it.

♥LjS

Message of the Moment:

If you're feeling uncomfortable right now, good!

It's only when you begin to feel uncomfortable can you be sure you're beginning to change, grow, evolve, etc.

Just ask a caterpillar and look what happens to it!

♥LjS

Message of the Moment:

Mastery of self not others

♥ LjS

Message of the Moment:

Be the light...for you are of it
Be the space…you are that too
You are the space in between the light...
You are everything
Know it
BE

♥LjS

Message of the Moment:

Don't judge for you never know when you'll walk in those shoes...
But you already know this, right?

♥ LjS

Message of the Moment:

Do what you love...for it's a part of YOU!

There's no right or wrong way to do the things you love.
If yourself is telling you from its quiet and balanced place,
"This is what you love", then go for it and accept no less.

Listen only to you. Listen to what you feel is to be the truth of you.

Don't worry about others and their wishes for you; it will work out for YOU.

Don't worry about your stuff for that doesn't matter,
It's just S T U F F.

When you sit in quiet contemplation, what happens?
How do you feel?
What answers do you get?

Shut out the outside world and listen to the sound of YOU...

FEEL THE WORD:

ME
ME
ME

Feels strange to say, yet at the same time, comforting

Say, feel, and think of only
ME ME ME ME ME ME..........Hmmmmmmmmmmmm......
OMMMMMMMMM...... MEEEEEEEEEEE

Feel the vibration of the word "ME"
It vibrates so high because it's you!

♥ LjS

Message of the Moment:

Health is wealth

Don't wait until you are poor to know this

♥LjS

Message of the Moment:

The truth always comes out

♥LjS

Message of the Moment:

_____

(Sometimes there's just nothing left to say)

♥LjS

Message of the Moment:

Tilt your head to gain a different perspective!

What you're looking at will not change...

The way you look at it will.

EASY RIGHT???

♥LjS

Message of the Moment:

Sleep, rest, be well, and know that all is good.

♥LjS

Message of the Moment:

What are your days, and even your weeks, going to look like?

YOU decide!

Choose to make it happen and remember,
"Your wish is my command".

♥LjS

Message of the Moment:

Everyone has a story?

Start thinking about yours...

I bet it's a good one to share!

♥LjS

Message of the Moment:

There is the pressure of *getting it right* the first time
to avoid the consequences of *not getting it right* the second time.

There's no right...there's no wrong...

Make a decision, live in your truth, and let the rest fall where it may.

Hey, we're all doing the best we can, even you.

♥ LjS

Message of the Moment:

SMILE...

Even if only for a second

You'll feel better

♥ LjS

Message of the Moment:

Seeds...

Plant your seeds, create and design the garden you want, nurture your dreams and, make it happen.

If you're not ready to receive don't bother!

P.S. You have to know you're worth it to create it in the first place.

Think about that for a second or two.

♥ LjS

Message of the Moment:

If you think you're doing it alone....think again!

YOU would never be "here" alone.

YOU have your own team of peeps all around you, helping pull you through, guiding you, and sending you PURE LOVE always.

It's all about you today and everyday.

They are there for you.

Ask and you shall receive!

♥LjS

Message of the Moment:

Be a:

BAD ASS, ROCK STAR, SPIRITUAL, WARRIOR, GODDESS (GOD)
Courage, strength, perseverance, will power, awareness, self-love...

♥LjS

Message of the Moment:

Why do you let people get to you?
Because you're not living for you, you're living for them.

Life is short; some people will like you...some people will not....some people
will have your back...some people will not, does it matter?

I bet you'll find that when you look at what you do have, and who you have in
your life, you'll find you're the luckiest person ever.

Live and prosper by the laws of the universe...

They're designed for YOU!

♥ LjS

Message of the Moment:

Stop, Rewind, Re-record then Rewind again, NOW hit Play

Does the past REALLY exist????

I'm thinking not so much!

It's the tapes the mind plays over, and over, and over again
that makes us believe it does.

If you're going to have tapes play, make sure they're the tapes of what you
want them to say, not the ones you don't!

Time to get to work

Stop, Rewind, Re-record then Rewind again, NOW hit Play

♥ LjS

Message of the Moment:

What's your moment telling you?

♥ LjS

Message of the Moment:

No is not an answer for you.

You know yourself better than anyone else.

YOU know what works and what will best for YOU!

Trust it.

Stop being afraid of what other people say.

♥LjS

Message of the Moment:

We all need to know that life is short.

REALLY SHORT.

Don't wait for tomorrow.

Don't put off doing ANYTHING that you want to do....

So cliché yet guided to tell you this again, until you KNOW it.

♥LjS

Message of the Moment:

My mantra for you,

"Do it *your* way and the rest will fall into place".

Why?

Because your way is simply YOUR way
and it's perfect the way you create it to be.

Don't waste a moment of your life doing it the way
others want you to do it.

Be beautiful today and shine for the entire world to see.

It's meant to be YOUR way.

You created it, now live it.

SHOW UP and SHINE

♥LjS

Message of the Moment:

Worth repeating:

Expectations are disappointments in the making.

Expect nothing and be joyfully surprised by everything.

Same thing for attachments…

♥LjS

Message of the Moment:

Simply said...

Have fun whatever that is for you.

Most people don't do that enough.

♥LjS

Message of the Moment:

Find solace in music…

It heals the soul with its vibration.

♥ LjS

Message of the Moment:

New rule…

"You're either on Team _____ (enter team name here) or you're not. If you're not on my team, then I'm sure there's another team that'll fit your needs".

Create your moments, your team, and make it your way...
After all no one else can tell you how to play *your* game.

Smile and know that you're loved.

All players will be provided for you,
All you have to do is just ask.

♥LjS

Message of the Moment:

Blank sheets of paper become tomorrow's dreams.

Let go of the old pages for they were pages out of your old book.

They have no place in the now.

You have new blank sheets to create this moment the way
YOU want them to be created.

Close the book on the old issues and on the past.
Don't allow or write them on your new blank sheets for tomorrow.

Ideas are yours...live them.
The days are yours…create them.
Create them and so it shall be…you have work to do.

LjS

Message of the Moment:

There's a lot of wisdom in the clouds

♥LjS

Message of the Moment:

Not all victories are about winning,
they're usually about the struggle, and always about the journey.

The only way to win is *to do,* not to *do not.*

♥LjS

Message of the Moment:

If an "idea" comes to you out of no where, it's coming to you for a reason.

Some part of you has created this thought or idea to get your attention.

This "idea" or thought is something that you've come up with for one reason or another.

Pay attention, explore, and determine its message.

Follow up, act, and see where the magic carpet ride takes you!

♥LjS

Message of the Moment:

View
Detach
Witness
Observe

See with different eyes.

That's how you change your perspective to change your life.

♥LjS

Message of the Moment:

Today is your day

Do with it what you will

It's yours and only yours

It's your gift

It's yours to create and make good or bad

It's a new decade, New Year, new moment

Be within it and allow yourself to feel it

Again, the day is created for YOU!

♥LjS

Message of the Moment:

Be the new in the year
Be the light in the sky
Be the beauty that you admire
Be the melody in the music
Be the color in the canvas
And remember, everything is always new again.

♥LjS

Message of the Moment:

One joy scatters a hundred griefs.
Chinese Proverb

♥LjS

Message of the Moment:

Don't let anyone take your power, therefore the you of you.

It's *your* power not *their* power.

You're perfect and divine just the way you are.

Not everyone is going to get you all the time.

That's ok,

BE YOU!

If nothing else, you'll be happy!

♥LjS

Message of the Moment:

No one really cares what you do in the long run...

the only person really affected by your choice and decision is you.

Choose wisely.

♥LjS

Message of the Moment:

So simple if we feel…

So complicated when we think...

Smile even though things might not be going so good...

The one thing you can always count is on YOU to make it better.

Don't be scared...keep it simple.

You're OK!

♥ LjS

Message of the Moment:

Let it all go...see what happens.

♥LjS

Message of the Moment:

When you least expect miracles...

Just in the nick of time...

When all hope is gone...

They appear!

That's why they're called miracles.

♥LjS

Message of the Moment:

There's only one act of unconditional love that's needed to take the place of a 100, or a 1000, or a 1,000,000 wrong doings.

We have this amazing innate ability to forgive and love.

Open your hearts and be willing to accept,

then your spirit will be set free.

♥LjS

Message of the Moment:

Act from your heart.

Give because that's what you do.

Let the love in.

Share!

Love is all of ours EQUALLY.

Allow it to flow where it needs to go.

Love does not need us to tell it where to go, it just knows.

♥LjS

Message of the Moment:

Sometimes you just have to say you're sorry and leave it at that...

LjS

Message of the Moment:

We dislike the things we don't understand because they scare us.

There comes the inevitable time when there's no room for FEAR..

Our teacher will appear to show us what we don't know or understand.

DEAL WITH IT!

It was at your request.

♥LjS

Message of the Moment:

You're only as old as you think you are.

How many years young are you anyway?

♥LjS

Message of the Moment:

Sit quietly in the chaos...

Find peace in your heart...

Remember that you have the choice on how you want to

RE-ACT

Be the change...

YOU have the power to do this

YOU REALLY DO!

♥LjS

Message of the Moment:

Sometimes it's only when we are bent, almost to the point of breaking, do we learn the value and strength of WHO WE ARE, and finally see what we're really made of.

Think of a palm tree...

Bendable, not breakable, even during the strongest of storms.
Be the palm tree

♥LjS

Message of the Moment:

Transformation and change...

Give yourself permission to be ok with the things and people that no longer
serve you.

Growth is about change.

Change is about the need for more.

We're here to continually evolve.

People and situations are here to assist (a.k.a test) our process.

Trust the universe and trust your higher self.

With the intention of self love, not fear, you will rise to great heights.

LjS

Message of the Moment:

Sometimes the greatest gifts are the ones that we never see

They show up like a gentle wind

Swirling in the air until the gifts move through you

Leaving behind the freshness of a new day

♥LjS

Message of the Moment:

RISE
UP

Meet your challenges don't allow them to meet you.

Rise high and free above all the *stuff* that holds you back
from soaring into your sweetest dreams.

RISE
ABOVE

♥LjS

Message of the Moment:

Be who you are because if you're not you, then who are you?

Who else can possibly be you?

♥LjS

Message of the Moment:

If you're not being honest with yourself,
how can anyone else be honest with you?

♥ LjS

Message of the Moment:

Time for you to kick some butt today.

What will another day of time really get you if you wait until tomorrow?

Answer: The same thing as today

♥LjS

Message of the Moment:

Do you really think you have all the answers?

Amazing that we think do.
Truth is we're only at the very tip of the iceberg because that is all we can see.

Life and nature are amazing.

No-thing really is what we think it is...most things exist underneath the surface
only showing you the peak

Open up, see, feel, explore, and go deep.

Be the above and the below.
Be the answers that you seek.

As above so below

♥LjS

Message of the Moment:

Believe in YOU

That's all that is asked of you

The rest will fall into place, easily, with little effort

TRUST the process

The design of *us* is brilliant

♥LjS

Message of the Moment:

Let it all be

Let your EGO go

Stop fighting it

Rest easy knowing that *all* is only just right now

♥ LjS

Message of the Moment:

Accepting and forgiving the past
is the only way to move into the future with an open heart.

Hey, sometimes it just was what it was!

♥LjS

Message of the Moment:

Silence, stillness, and love;

That's your homework for the day

♥ LjS

Message of the Moment:

Never question why you did or didn't do something.

When you think about it,
could you really have done any better or different at *that* time?

Probably not or you would have.

Be nice to yourself.

♥LjS

Message of the Moment:

Move like nature
bend with the wind
ground like the tree
fly like the bird
be the bee
and flow like the water...

♥LjS

Message of the Moment:

Don't be afraid to change...you're doing it whether you know or not.

Fear wants you to stay the same.

Rise up to love.

♥LjS

Message of the Moment:

Be who you are for YOU

Don't be something you're not because you think
someone wants you to be that

YOU are YOU!

BEAUTIFUL, WONDERFUL and LOVED

ALWAYS

Tired of hearing this yet…I hope not!

♥LjS

Message of the Moment:

SPEAK truth

LIVE well

BE beautiful

DO it!

♥LjS

Message of the Moment:

Always let go of your dreams.

Allow the wind to take them wherever they need to be in the highest and best.

Don't be surprised if they come back, different, yet better than you could've ever initially dreamt.

♥ LjS

Message of the Moment:

Smile like you own the world,
it was created for you.

LjS

Message of the Moment:

POWER

Your power is your birthright

USE IT TO CREATE CHANGE

♥LjS

Message of the Moment:

Perseverance

The key to all your dreams coming true.

♥LjS

Message of the Moment:

There's a lot the dark can teach you,
usually more than the light.

♥ LjS

Message of the Moment:

Affirmation:

"In this moment, I am whole and I am complete in my physical, emotional, mental, and spiritual bodies...

In this moment, I am whole and I am complete in my physical, emotional, mental, and spiritual bodies...

.

In this moment, I am whole and I am complete in my physical, emotional, mental, and spiritual bodies...."

♥LjS

Message of the Moment:

Don't be afraid to try new things, new situations,
and step out of your *familiar* comfort zone.

If it weren't for the new, there would be no old.

LjS

Message of the Moment:

Stop trying to figure it out...

IT DOESN'T MATTER!

♥ LjS

Message of the Moment:

It's all the about the "I" today.

The letter "U" can wait until tomorrow.

♥ LjS

Message of the Moment:

When you turn the "WE" upside down you empty it out and
then you're left with "ME"

♥LjS

Message of the Moment:

TRUST...

♥LjS

Message of the Moment:

No one ever dies...we all just eventually change form.

An ice cube turns to liquid and then it evaporates.
This is a metaphor for the physical body.

When it evaporates, where does it go?

It's not gone here or there, it has gone everywhere.

We're everywhere, *all* the time, in everything, always.

No one ever leaves you so don't allow let the physical separation fool you!

♥LjS

Message of the Moment:

You're perfectly imperfect...

That's part of the beauty of life.

Perfection is an illusion.

Imperfection is a beautiful reality.

♥ LjS

Message of the Moment:

Strength and Perseverance

You're created with these in you as a part of who you are.

Be open to see them inside yourself.

Recognize them to become aware of them and then allow what you have within you to do its thing.

It's already done.

♥LjS

Message of the Moment:

Sometimes we all need a little help from our friends.

Know that when you can't find them,
and no one seems to be offering you a hand,
you'll be provided for in another way.

♥ LjS

Message of the Moment:

ACTIONS CREATE RESULTS

Move through the action,

Create the results,

Never settle for no,

Discover the results.

♥LjS

Message of the Moment:

CHANGES!

Imagine warm water gently entering through the top of your head and exiting out the center of your forehead.

As it leaves, it takes with it all the old *stuff* you no longer need and what is not serving you any longer.

Ahhhh

SWEET and GENTLE
RELEASE

Now allow the new water to bring in what you need.

♥ LjS

Message of the Moment:

Choices...word of the day to dig into.

We all have them yet most of us will argue we don't.

What we're really saying is we don't like the choices we have to choose from, so it's easier to say we don't have any at all.

The fact is when it comes to making a choice; making the choice itself can be worse than dealing with the choice you chose.

A consequence is the natural result of any choice, not good or bad, just a consequence...maybe that's the word for tomorrow.

LjS

Message of the Moment:

You can try all you want but sometimes trying is not enough.

Other people have free will, their own journey, and their own baggage.

Live for you, own *your* stage, and be the rock star *you* were born to be.

Let others choose their own stage.

You can't be on two stages at once.

♥LjS

Message of the Moment:

No time...

No Space...

ANYTHING IS POSSIBLE

♥LjS

Message of the Moment:

Messages are everywhere
in everything
always for
YOU!

♥ LjS

Message for the Moment:

Let bygone's be bygone's,
Let the past be where it is,
Allow freedom and movement into the present,
Allow the future to develop at its own pace,
Co create with all that is,
Act on what feels right,
Express yourself in the way that best suits you,
ALWAYS hold your head up high, love yourself,
and BE PROUD of all that you are, and all that you have ever been.

Never let anyone take your power again.
You have this...I know you do!

Say, "I got this".

♥LjS

Message of the Moment:

Do the best you can, know where you are within yourself and your personal truths, decide what works best for YOU, decide to be happy, accept life for what it is and is not, allow people to love you, don't be afraid, follow your path not that of others, be brave and beautiful, never ever allow those who want to scare you or hurt you do so, don't let others take your energy or show up to take you off track.

Own your power, own your voice, own your space, own your truths, own your choices, and own your life.

The time is in this moment.

♥LjS

Message of the Moment:

At the end of your life,
you'll find the only competition that existed was with yourself.

♥LjS

Message of the Moment:

SIMPLICITY...

Takes you a long way if you let it!

♥ LjS

Message of the Moment:

There's only so much that can be said.

It's only until *you* decide that you've had enough,
will you change what needs to be changed.

A warrior doesn't go into battle saying he surrenders,
and then keeps charging ahead.

Either you surrender to what is or you keep moving forward.
You can't do both, regardless of what you say to yourself and others.

There's only one truth with this.

When you have had enough, you'll surrender and accept what is, and then you
can allow what will be.

Until then, you will remain in battle.

♥LjS

Message of the Moment:

Be beautiful
Know you're safe
Stand proud
Take what is
That is courage

♥LjS

Message of the Moment:

Homework:

Start writing your own,
"Declaration of Independence"

How do your want *your* country to run?

What do you want it to look like?

What will you accept and what will you not accept?

What are your boundaries?
What are the laws?
Who is in charge?

Declare yourself

♥LjS

Message of the Moment:

WRITE, WRITE, WRITE
DANCE, DANCE, DANCE
PAINT, PAINT, PAINT
SING, SING, SING
LAUGH, LAUGH, LAUGH
LOVE, LOVE, LOVE

♥ LjS

Message of the Moment:

Rise up and greet each other.
High five, fist bump, and yell hello!
No one is ever alone.

♥LjS

Message of the Moment:

I have no answers.
Only you have the answers you seek.
All we can do for each other is connect, listen, guide, hold space,
and share what we know.
Call that what you want.

♥LjS

Message of the Moment:

If you keep doing the same thing over and over
expecting a different result…well, we all know how this one goes.

Yet, are you really paying attention to the end result?
If you were, I bet you wouldn't keep doing it.

Only *you* can stop the crazy train.
Knowing that you have this *power* is very empowering.

♥ LjS

Message of the Moment:

Sometimes you just have to try harder than you do on other days.

♥ LjS

Message of the Moment:

Nothing changes until you change...

SIMPLE

You must do the work.

♥LjS

Message of the Moment:

The world is your mirror.
In any given moment it will reflect back to you, yourself.

It shows you exactly what you need to look at and examine at that time for your greater good.

Don't be afraid, hurt, bothered, let down, disappointed, heart broken, frustrated or sad by this.

It's just a reflection of the moment.
Detach and witness yourself as you evolve and grow.

When you witness; see, examine, and determine what you need to take away from its reflection and move on.

If not, you'll get trapped within it.

I've done both.

I like to witness and examine as much as possible.

♥ LjS

Message of the Moment:

Inspire those who look for inspiration, speak with those who seek truth, laugh with those who know humor, and love all regardless of everything else.

♥LjS

Message of the Moment:

We all get stuck in the separation.

It's how we remember our *individual unity* that matters.

No judgment is the truth of all that is.

♥LjS

Message of the Moment:

This too shall pass...time is a beautiful gift.

♥LjS

Message of the Moment:

Take nothing for granted.

It could all be gone when you wake up and everything will different.

♥LjS

Message of the Moment:

Temporary weakness from the extreme
(working out, emotional distress, mental exhaustion, etc.)
with the proper care, nurturing, and self love...
will lead to greater strength tomorrow!

♥LjS

Message of the Moment:

To bad complaining doesn't fix anything.

If it did, we would *all* be living in Disney World!

♥LjS

Message of the Moment:

No excuses...no regrets

LjS

Message of the Moment:

If you start to pay attention to the details of your own life,
you'll be amazed by what the details are trying to tell you.

PAY ATTENTION as you weave your story.

The ending is up to you.

♥LjS

Message of the Moment:

What's your "Message of the Moment"?

_____
_____
_____
_____
_____
_____
_____
_____
_____
_____
_____
_____
_____
_____
_____
_____
_____

♥ YoU

Message of the Moment:

YOUR life is YOURS

Live, be, and do what YOU enjoy because at the end of YOUR life no one gives a damn but YOU!

♥LjS

Message of the Moment:

Today, I want you to drink a glass of water different than you do on other days.

As you're drinking this glass of water, I want you to give thanks for just that one glass of water you're drinking *today* and nothing else.

If everyone did that, with just that one glass of water *today*, can you imagine how much gratitude and love would go out to the world, in only one day?

♥LjS

Message of the Moment:

The sand bags holding you down today
are preventing you from taking off tomorrow.

They need to be cut in order to fly.

Fly free, fly away, and fly wherever you want...
The sky is your pallet and the balloon is your brush.

Scissors anyone?
It's time to paint and it's time for you to fly.

♥LjS

Message of the Moment:

Complications

Do we make them?
Does life just happen?

Maybe they're not complications?
Maybe they're about something else?

Complications....

♥LjS

Message of the Moment:

Remember, it's all just an experience!

♥ LjS

Message of the Moment:

There's so much that is being missed everywhere in everything.

If we would allow, listen, and accept something other than our (self limiting) narrow beliefs, we would be able to not only benefit ourselves, we would help each other, therefore changing the world to that of greater healing.

We're here to help each other as we personally evolve
(one change can't help but change the whole)
and lead the world to greater consciousness of all that is.

♥LjS

Message of the Moment:

We say we want to "give and be of service".

If you want to be of service then be of service.

It's not about wanting to do something,
it's about being humble, showing up, and doing it!

It's not about wanting to do it; it's just do-ing.

Service!

♥LjS

Message of the Moment:

Affirmation:

"Patience & Wisdom are two of my best friends. They never leave me alone, they always do things to make sure I remember them; they serve my greatest good even when I don't want them too, and they always have my back. Their love is unconditional and I am grateful to have them with me at all times, regardless of how I am feeling at the moment. Thank you for all that's available to help, love, and guide me through all of my days....and so it is".

♥LjS

Message of the Moment:

Pedestals

Often we have these pre-conceived notions who and what people are, or are not.

Frequently, we want them to be the way we *want* them to be and we put them on a pedestal high above ourselves.

By doing this, it fills our own void so we can see ourselves in something, or someone, other than ourselves.

What's wrong with being who we are?

You give away your power when you put others on a pedestal and take theirs away since they have no where to go but down.

Stand alone and proud on your own pedestal
and allow others their glory as well.

♥LjS

Message of the Moment:

"WHAT" one gives is not as important as "HOW" one gives.

The "HOW'S" carry the intention and the intention carries the message.

The intention is unconsciously what's received by the recipient...
therefore the "HOW" is actually what's given, not the "WHAT".

Anyone can give money, things, and stuff,
yet can anyone give, what we really all want, which is what is given in the
"HOW"?

What do you want your "WHAT" to say?

Say it with your "HOW"!

♥LjS

Message of the Moment:

If you want to be respected, then you must be respectful.

You get what you put out.

It may take awhile, yet it's the universal law.

Be good to others because in the end no one will care whether you were good or not, but you.

Everything ends where it all began...with *you*!

♥LjS

Message of the Moment:

ALIGN:

*A*llowing *L*ove *I*nside *G*rowing *N*aturally

♥LjS

Message of the Moment:

Either you're losing your mind or finding your heart.

Maybe you need to do one to gain the other.

♥ LjS

Message of the Moment:

If the Phoenix can raise so can you.

Now get up!

♥LjS

Message of the Moment:

How's it possible that something as small as a bird, which can fit in the palm of your hand, can sing as loud and powerful as it does?

Because no one ever told it that it couldn't!

♥LjS

Message of the Moment:

Let your intention guide your sleigh

♥LjS

Message of the Moment:

How can an animal love us so much with no judgment, no expectations, and so much unconditional love?

We must be doing something right in our lives to get a million pounds of LOVE from 9 lbs of life!

♥LjS

Message of the Moment:

Knowing that nothing and no one ever *dies*,
knowing that nothing is what we *think* it is,
knowing that even though we may *not know* what's in store for us,
knowing that whatever we think we *know and want* is never nearly as awesome
as what we end up receiving, is astounding.

By the way, that doesn't mean that life doesn't scare the hell out of us now and
then.

We're here to be human after all.
Uncertainty is part of humanity and *can* be scary.

I do know this much though;
You, we, all of us, are loved beyond what we can comprehend love to be.

♥LjS

Message of the Moment:

Warning:

Emotional roller coasters, whether by yourself or with others, can leave you feeling turned around and upside down.

Do *not* get on if you don't want to ride.

If you get on, remember that's your choice and no one is making you ride.

If you choose to ride, you better put your seatbelt on.

They don't call it a roller coaster for nothing.

♥ LjS

Message of the Moment:

You are what you believe you are.

What do you believe today?

You can be anything that you want?

♥LjS

Message of the Moment:

DON'T LOOK DOWN

♥ LjS

Message of the Moment:

When you love
Love with all your heart
That's what love really is anyway

♥LjS

Message of the Moment:

"Peace Takes Courage"

Peace also takes strength, acceptance, perseverance, be-ing, tolerance, self-love and compassion.

Peace is Courage

♥ LjS

Message of the Moment:

YOU, I, WE are not defined by *what* YOU, I, WE do.

YOU, I, WE, are defined by *who* YOU, I, WE, is.

Understanding what defines you will save you a lot of inner turmoil.

If you're defining yourself by what you do,
you're missing it all BIG time.

♥LjS

Message of the Moment:

Choices
Options
Selections

They're always there whether you like them or not.

You can't argue that.

You can however argue about the choices you have.

Either way, they're there.

♥LjS

Message of the Moment:

I know first hand that those who hurt us the most...love us the most.

It doesn't make sense I know...but I promise you one day it will.

In the meantime, believe nothing and no one is what you think they are...everything is always *so* much more.

This is where you'll find the answers that you seek.

♥LjS

Message of the Moment:

It's ok to be still.
It's ok to be tired.
It's ok to not know.
The answers will come.

It's within the silence we can hear the most.

♥LjS

Message of the Moment:

Let the bad fish go...they just end up smelling up the entire basket!

♥ LjS

Message of the Moment:

What you think of me is frankly none of my business.

What I think of you is none of yours.

Your business is only yours and others is only theirs.

We know this, yet for some reason we have such a hard time
staying in our own cup.

♥LjS

Message of the Moment:

I went for a bike ride through a cemetery.

On one side of the path there was a headstone with the last name,
"FEAR".

On the other side of the path, directly facing it was the last name,
"STRONG".

What are the chances? I wonder if anyone else ever has noticed that on either
side of the path.

Today, that was my message of the moment.
I always love how spirit works.
K*no*w Coincidences!

What are your messages from spirit today?
Where are you finding them?

Probably in the most unlikely, yet most obvious of places!

♥LjS

Message of the Moment:

From what I keep seeing and hearing, these are some of the things the most successful people have in common:

They stopped caring what other people thought of them, they stopped being afraid of rejection, they turned negatives into positives, they stopped listening to other people who didn't share the same vision, they kept going, and they listened to their inner knowing, a.k.a. their gut.

Finally, they trusted themselves!

The formula for success for you is this:
Simply everything you already have, and everything you always have been, lives right inside you, to succeed in whatever you want, and it's in the knowing that you are, and always have been, a huge success.

Do you have what it takes?

Of course you do!

♥LjS

Message of the Moment:

Strength works

♥LjS

Message of the Moment:

"Staying in the flow of all that is"

This reminds me of the whitewater rafting trip I went on years ago
with my family.

Life is like a river...it guides you, has twists and turns, follows its own path that
it has carved, and continues to carve, out of the banks that hold it together.
It's beautiful and shallow, yet can be very deep in some spots. It can be clean
or polluted depending how we treat it, nourishing or depleting, and has both
rough and calm waters depending where you are in it.

Rivers bring all sorts of ups and downs, ins and outs, surprises, beautiful
scenery, and sometimes not so beautiful moments.

The best we can do is wear our safety gear, listen to what our "guides" tell us
to do while rafting, sit upright in our boat, hunker down, find our balance,
paddle through the rough water, stay focused, and then finally rest when we
made it through the rapids to calmer waters.

The river always brings new adventures, around each bend, as life often does.
Both are beautiful, magical, can be harsh, and rarely understood. They're not
meant to be questioned only to be a part of, respected, and enjoyed.

A river is just being a river, our job is to take it all in, do the best we can, use
the tools that we have to paddle through the rough spots,
and float when things are calm.

Before you know it...the view will change again. Soon it'll be time for a new
bend in the "river". All we can do is enjoy the ride and let it happen.

Go with flow comes to mind....

♥LjS

279

Message of the Moment:

We all have different journeys and experiences.

Positive thoughts are great and sound good,
yet divine order sometimes is greater.

Some things we'll never understand.

We must have faith to trust all is as it needs to be,
and maybe the healing is in the "illness" itself,
not only in the healing we think we want and receive.

♥LjS

Message of the Moment:

The webs of our lives together, the places we have been apart, the smallest
details of each of our lives, and the situations and places
we find ourselves in today, all tell a great story.

The story of you...
The story of me...

The story of all of us unified by nature into one,
and separated by our humanity into billions of beings.

Allow the story we're all writing to write itself, while you follow the bread
crumbs of your life, all while allowing others to follow theirs.

You'll be amazed at where you find yourself and how your story is connected
to all of ours.

 LjS

Message of the Moment:

If you sit too long in a dirty smelly porta potty, you won't even realize it's dirty and stinky anymore.

Why? Because you'll become so accustomed to the stench and filth,
you won't even know it's there.
Hard to believe but true!

Sometimes it takes someone else's perspective to reawaken your senses. Then when you get this new perspective, you wonder why you were not seeing (or in this case smelling) it yourself all along.

I suppose we just get used to the way things are and
we become numb to what is.

That's a little survival feature we were equipped with on this little trip to Earth. If not, we would be jumping out of our skin all the time and we would miss everything we need to know all together.

Thank goodness for others and their wake up calls to keeps us on our toes. Don't be angry with others for taking you out of the porta potty. Most likely, they'll have to do it while you're kicking and screaming (because you like your comfort zone).

Those who love you will do it for you anyway.
They can see for you when you can not!

♥ LjS

One Moment at a Time
Messages Just for Today

O.M.A.A.T

One Moment at a Time
Messages Just for Today

For today, I am grateful for all that I have, all that I receive, and all that I shall give.

Today, I know the difference between:

~Good and evil
~Up and down
~Yes and no
~Positive and negative
~Black and white
~Wants and needs
~Reality and illusion
~Me and you

Today, I understand that not everything will go *my* way. Things will go the way they *need* to go in order for my soul to develop and my spirit to soar

Today, I will be me. I will stay in peace and I will do my best to be who I am

Today, I will not hurt myself, I will not speak poorly about myself, and I will not abuse my body

Today, I will lead by example and fall asleep proud of the person that I was all day

Today, I will tell someone I love them

Today, I will find compassion for those who are in the most pain

Today, I will fill my vessel first and then fill the vessel of others if so asked

Today, I will walk with my head high

Today, I will serve and be served

Today, I will worship and be worshiped

Today, I will love and be loved

Today, I will allow what is rightfully mine to come to me with ease

Today, I will not cry for what was lost but rejoice in what I have found

Today, I will not have guilt, since I will know for today, that we all make choices and that other people's choices are not a reflection upon me

Today, I will not let people take my power or take the power of others

Today, I will be grateful for what I do and do not have

Today, I will find forgiveness for myself

Today, I will find forgiveness for one other person

Today, I will heal

Today, I will use my voice

Today, I will be strong

Today, I will bend

Today, I will persevere

Today, I will not care if you like me

Today, I will not care what is said about me

Today, I will hold my head up high and be proud

Today, I will remember my truth

Today, I will take a long shower

Today, I will listen to the birds sing

Today, I will sing out loud

Today, I will know my inner beauty

Today, I will *know* that I am *never* alone

Today, I will know that nothing is what I think it is

Today, I will know I am not a victim of anything or anyone

Today, I will *know* I have choices

Today, I will feel my freedom

Today, I will be a friend to myself as well as others

Today, I will see myself the way others see me

Today, I will open my heart

Today, I will be honest…with myself as well as others

Today, I will be healthy...in all of my bodies

Today, I will not be angry with me or with you

Today, I will let the past be the past

Today, I will see the others persons perspective and not let it influence my own

Today, I will not project how I feel onto others or allow others to project onto me

Today, I will be still

Today, I will be my own guru

Today, I will not be afraid

Today, I will know my talent

Today, I will know my worth

Today, I will take care of me

Today, I will remember to breathe

Today, I will call someone to say, "I love you" or "I'm thinking of you" or "I just wanted to call and say hello" and mean it from my heart to theirs

Today, I am grateful for what I do have

Today, I will understand and *know* that nothing and no one can ever die

Today, I will stay in my moment

Today, I will know all my needs are being met

Today, I will *know* I AM A ROCK STAR baby

Today, I will be proud of where I came from, where I am today, and where I am heading tomorrow

Today will just be another day…

Totally
Opening
Doors
Allowing
Yesterday to be yesterday and today to be today

Lisa J. Smith

About the Author

Lisa J. Smith, also known as "The New Voice for a New Age", is a well-known intuitive, medium, empowerment speaker, and author.

She is the mother of two grown children and the mom to two cats. Lisa J. resides in the suburbs of Detroit, MI and has lived there for all of her life.

Lisa is known for her practical, honest, real, and down to earth approach. Her unique delivery, her positive attitude, her approachable girl next-door charm, and her down to earth messages are quickly touching lives of people all over the world.

Lisa works with her clients, listeners, and audience members in a unique way so as to touch their soul and help heal their hearts. Her positive, and sometimes humorous outlook, is changing the way people around the world view themselves and others even through the toughest of times.

As Lisa J. says, "Wherever in the world you are, I am too".

Peeps Publishing
PP
www.peepspublishing.com

Find Lisa J. Smith at:

www.facebook.com/lisajsmithfans

www.twitter.com/lisajsmith

www.lisajsmith.com

4240400R00176

Made in the USA
San Bernardino, CA
07 September 2013